S0-BAJ-192

American Jazz

Scott Joplin

Russell Roberts

Mitchell Lane
PUBLISHERS
P.O. Box 196
Hockessin, Delaware 19707

American JAZZ

Benny Goodman
Bessie Smith
Billie Holiday
Charlie Parker
Count Basie
Dizzy Gillespie
Louis Armstrong
Miles Davis
Ornette Coleman
Scott Joplin

PUBLISHER'S NOTE: The facts on which this book is based have been thoroughly researched. Documentation of such research can be found on page 45. While every possible effort has been made to ensure accuracy, the publisher will not assume liability for damages caused by inaccuracies in the data, and makes no warranty on the accuracy of the information contained herein.

Printing 1 2 3 4 5 6 7 8 9

Library of Congress Cataloging-in-Publication Data

Roberts, Russell, 1953–
Scott Joplin / by Russell Roberts.
pages cm — (American jazz)
Includes bibliographical references and index.
ISBN 978-1-61228-273-2 (library bound)
1. Joplin, Scott, 1868–1917—Juvenile literature.
2. Composers—United States—Biography—Juvenile literature. I. Title.
ML3930.J66R63 2013
780.92—dc23
[B]

2012008633

eBook ISBN: 9781612283494

PLB

Contents

Chapter 1

Treemonisha

Musical composer Scott Joplin sat down at the piano in the theater on this day in 1911 and looked up at the stage. The performers standing there stared back at him. Each held many pieces of paper that contained the words and music of an opera called *Treemonisha* that Joplin had written.

"We're ready, Mr. Joplin," one of the performers, a young black man, said. The other men and women nodded in agreement. Some of them had butterflies in their stomach. They looked down at the floor for a second to calm their nerves. They knew it was perhaps the biggest night in Joplin's life, and they didn't want to let him down.

One of the performers looked out at the audience. Although this theater, which was located in Harlem, could hold many people, not a lot of seats were filled. The performer quickly counted the people he saw: 17.[1] He shook his head sadly. This small crowd was almost certainly bad news for Joplin.

He looked down at Joplin sitting at the piano. Joplin was an African-American man in his mid-forties. He had a neat appearance; his hair was short and he grew neither beard nor mustache. From working with him the performer knew that Joplin was a quiet man. Although he played the piano, and piano players tended to be flamboyant, Joplin never showed off. He was serious—almost too serious—about what he did, and what he did was write music. He was very, very good at that.

Joplin had already achieved fame and success for his ragtime songs—popularly known as rags—and in early-twentieth-century America, fame and success were not easy for African Americans to come by. Slavery was still fresh in many people's minds—the Civil War had ended barely fifty years before—and some people still looked down on African Americans.

Joplin, though, had risen above the prejudice and disdain because of his extraordinary talent. As one of the pioneers of ragtime, songs with his name attached to them often found a favorable reaction with the music-loving public.

This production was different, however. Joplin was not introducing a new ragtime song tonight, but rather a three-act opera entitled *Treemonisha.*

Joplin bent over the piano slightly, and his fingers started dancing over the keys. Piano music soared through the theater; it filled the dusty corners and rattled the window glass.

The performers glanced down at the sheets of paper in their hands. Some of them began to sing. Their voices rang throughout the theater. At the piano, Joplin smiled.

Treemonisha was an extremely ambitious work. At this time in the United States, many people thought African Americans couldn't write something as complicated as an opera.

If anyone could prove how wrong that type of thinking was, it was Scott Joplin. He had come east from the Midwestern United States, and was already known as ragtime's greatest composer. His "Maple Leaf Rag" was one of the most popular rags of all time.

Yet Joplin had far greater things in mind than being known for just his rags. He had always wanted to write a successful opera.

Treemonisha was about an African-American girl whose mother's name was Monisha. The girl loved to sit under a special tree, so she was called Treemonisha. The people who lived around Treemonisha were former slaves. They had not gone to school. They believed magic was real. A man used this belief to scare them. He was able to steal money from them because the people thought he would use his magic against them if they tried to stop him. But Treemonisha had been to school. She knew the man was lying, and she tried to show her people that the man was tricking them just to steal their money. At first they didn't believe her, but she finally convinced them. The point of the opera was that African Americans needed an education. Joplin strongly believed in this message.

With 27 songs, *Treemonisha* was 230 pages long—very long indeed. In these days before recorded music, people would buy sheet music and play it on their home piano. Unfortunately, no one wanted to print a 230-page opera written by a black man. And if they did, it would be too expensive for most people to buy.

In the theater, Joplin scanned the audience. He hoped to see smiles, laughter, tears—anything to show that the small audience was interested in what was happening on stage.

Several people shifted in their seats. One man was sweating. He took off his hat and wiped his head with a handkerchief. Someone else coughed.

Joplin wondered, *Do they like it?* His fingers danced over the keys. Music filled the air. It echoed off the walls in the theater because there were so few people in attendance. On stage the performers sang and danced. Everyone was trying as hard as they could. But was it enough?

In the summer and autumn of 1910, Joplin had visited many music publishers with his opera, trying to get them to publish it. No one would. So, even though he did not have a lot of money, Joplin decided to pay to publish part of it himself. On May 19, 1911, the piano and vocal score for *Treemonisha* appeared for sale at $2.50 per copy. Joplin was hopeful people would like it and buy it, but that did not happen. He knew he needed something more to interest people in his opera.

At first he hoped someone would pay to produce *Treemonisha* on stage. Thomas Johnson planned to stage it in Atlantic City, New Jersey, but the show was canceled. Joplin decided to stage it himself. He didn't have costumes or scenery, and he didn't have an orchestra to play the

The spare 1911 production of *Treemonisha* received a favorable review in *The American Musician and Art Journal*, but it was not enough to generate interest in mounting a full production of the opera. It would not be staged during his lifetime.

music. All he had was himself on the piano and the performers on stage. He rented a theater in Harlem for one night and invited people to the show. He hoped one of them would pay to stage it properly.

Now the opera was almost over. Joplin was playing the final songs. The moment of truth was fast approaching.

He finished the final songs and leaned back, exhausted, on the piano stool. The last notes faded into nothingness.

The audience clapped and then got up from their seats. Some of the men came down to the piano. "Wonderful," they said, shaking Joplin's hand. "Superb."

"Thank you," Joplin replied, smiling. "Thank you." Maybe, just maybe, his gamble had paid off. His spirits soared and he was full of hope.

However, in the days and weeks that followed, no one came forward and offered to bankroll a production of *Treemonisha*. Joplin's optimism slowly faded as every day went by without the words he was hoping to hear.

He didn't know how else to get *Treemonisha* noticed. What was he going to do?

What Is Ragtime?

There are many different types of musical styles, including classical, jazz, country, folk, rap, and rock 'n roll. Ragtime is another musical style. For a while in America, ragtime was extremely popular.

Ragtime is hard to define, but it has roots in African-American music. It is a form of dance music with a syncopated melody played against a steady beat. (*Syncopated* means it has an altered beat pattern that interrupts the regular rhythm flow.) When people first heard this type of music, they thought it sounded "ragged." Even explained this way, however, the style is hard to define. Trying to figure out the origin of ragtime is like trying figure out which came first: the chicken or the egg.

Another explanation for the term *ragtime* is that the members of the bands that played this type of music wore rags (poor clothing). Yet another theory states that when bands were playing this type of music, a white rag was hung outside to signal that they were inside.

Even Scott Joplin, a master of ragtime, was not exactly clear how and why ragtime came to be. When he was asked to explain what ragtime music is, he said: "Oh, because it [the music] has such a ragged movement. It suggests something like that."[2]

Chapter 2

SCOTT JOPLIN

A Boy with a Gift

Florence put down her banjo and smiled at two-year-old Scott Joplin, who was sitting next to her. He was grinning from ear to ear. There was nothing he liked better than hearing his mother play her banjo.

Then Giles, Scott's father, picked up his fiddle and began to play. The fiddle bow danced and dipped as it moved over the strings. The music filled the house like a sweet smell. It floated through the air and out the windows. Anybody passing by this building on a northeast Texas farm near the town of Marshall in 1870 could hear the sweet sound of the music as it rolled over the landscape.

This was where Scott Joplin lived as a young boy. Sometimes his birthday is given as November 24, 1868, but this date is likely wrong. When there was a census taken (a census counts the number of people in an area) on July 18, 1870, it listed Joplin as being two years old.[1] This means that he was born earlier in 1868 than November. Maybe he was even born in 1867.

Scott's mother was Florence Givens. She was born in Kentucky about 1841. His father, Giles, was born in 1842 in North Carolina. The 1870 census listed the names and ages of the Joplin family as: Giles, 28; Florence, 29; Monroe, 9; Scott, 2; and Robert, 1.

By 1880 the Joplins had moved to Texarkana, a town on the border of Texas and Arkansas. By this time three more children had joined the family. For this census, Osie was 10; William, 4; and Myrtle, 3 months.[2]

Chapter 2

Music was in the Joplin blood, and everyone could see that Scott, even when young, had musical ability. By age seven he was playing the banjo. Several years later, Florence bought Scott an old piano. It wasn't much to look at, but it was all his. Scott sat down in front of it, ran his fingers over the keys, and thought he had never heard a nicer sound.

People around town gave Scott free music lessons to help him improve. One of those was a German man named Julius Weiss. He introduced Scott to classical European music. It was probably from Weiss that Joplin learned to love opera. Years later, Joplin still wrote letters to his old teacher. Sometimes he would even send him money.[3]

The sun was hot where Joplin lived. Especially in the summer, it was like a giant light bulb in the sky, beating down on everything in sight. It turned the ground dry and dusty, and made it hard to be outside. All anyone could think about was cooling off—maybe with a tall glass of water, or standing in the shade of a tree in a grassy meadow.

Scott probably thought about those things too. But he also thought about his music. He liked to think about what his life would be like when he was grown up and a big success in the music world. Alexander Ford, who knew Joplin at this time, said: "Scott worked on his music all the time. He was a musical genius. He didn't need a piece of music to go by. He played his own music without anything."[4]

At age sixteen, Scott formed a vocal group with several others in Texarkana, possibly including his brother Robert. He also played the piano in local dance halls and taught guitar and mandolin.

One day, when he was around twenty (some think it was earlier), Joplin decided to leave Texarkana. He knew that if he wanted to try to become a musician, he had to go to a bigger city. It was hard to leave his family and friends, but Joplin had a dream.

Some say that he traveled around until he settled in St. Louis, Missouri. Others think that he went to live in Sedalia, Missouri. (A 1903 issue of the newspaper *Sedalia Times* [after Joplin became famous] ran a headline reading: "Scott Joplin . . . was raised in Sedalia."[5])

As Joplin traveled he was like a sponge, soaking up all the music he heard. Each time he came to a town, he would go into a saloon,

A mural in Texarkana celebrates the time that Joplin lived in that city. Joplin attended the Orr School there, where many of his ideas and compositions took root.

restaurant, or nightclub where music was being played. As he listened to the music filtering through the smoky light, he would hear things most others wouldn't: how the beat changed, for instance, or how this or that type of instrument sounded. Eventually all these different musical ideas and styles would come tumbling back out of him.

Besides writing music, Joplin also played it wherever he went. However, because many people still looked down on African Americans, the places he could play were limited. Cheap bars were some of his only options.

A major event in both ragtime's history and Joplin's life occurred in 1893 at the Columbian Exposition in Chicago, also known as the World's Fair. The fair was extremely popular; millions of people went to it. A ring of saloons and gambling halls set themselves up just outside the fair. There, in the sawdust and the smoke, was where many black musicians, including Joplin, played their unique type of piano music, called ragtime. When the customers returned to their hometowns

Chapter 2

The Chicago World's Columbian Expo of 1893 celebrated the 400th anniversary of Columbus's discovery of America. Besides the new style of music, it featured a new way of delivering electricity (alternating current) and other marvelous inventions. It was also the first fair with rides and other attractions, including the original Ferris wheel. Built by George Ferris, it stood 264 feet (80 m) tall.

throughout America, they brought their love of ragtime with them. This was how ragtime spread across the United States.[6] Both ragtime and Scott Joplin were on the verge of making history.

Music and African Americans in the South

In the southern United States, music played an important role during slavery. When people from Africa were first brought to the New World, they were often separated from others in the same tribe. While slaves in many areas did not share a common language, members of different tribes could communicate through music, particularly by drumming on handmade drums. When slave owners took away the drums, the people continued to communicate by tapping their feet or clapping their hands in a certain way.

This rhythm system was also used when they sang songs while working in the fields. Since their hands and feet were busy, they used their voices. Singing while working made the long hours go faster. There were songs about work, songs about feelings, songs about religion—anything the workers wanted to express.

Music and song also became the slaves' way of spreading news. For example, many spirituals were sung to spread the word about the road to freedom from slavery.[7] Sometimes slave owners taught the slaves other types of music. The slaves added their own moans, cries, and other expressions to these songs.

The power of, and need for, music did not disappear with the end of slavery. Rather, it continued to play an important role in African-American homes. Scott Joplin's family was no different in its embrace of music.

Chapter 3
The
CRADLE OF
RAGTIME
SEDALIA MISSOURI

"Maple Leaf Rag"

Scott Joplin walked down the street in the town of Sedalia, Missouri. The sun was shining, and the air was warm and pleasant. From somewhere not too far away birds were singing from the leafy branches of a maple tree.

Something else filled the air too—music from a marching band. A little farther down the road the sound of music drifted from a building's open windows; it was a band practicing for a dance. A large sign on a corner announced an upcoming performance at the town's opera house.

Joplin smiled. He was in the right place—the "musical town of the West."[1]

Some of the music that Joplin heard in Sedalia was ragtime, for it was becoming popular all over. And just as ragtime was changing musical tastes, the United States was changing as well.

Americans were moving from farms to the cities. In 1890, when Joplin was in Sedalia, just 22 percent of the population lived in a town or city. Thirty years later, that figure would be 54 percent.[2] Although people still rode horses and used them for work such as pulling wagons, they were also now riding trains and streetcars, and automobiles were already on the horizon. Life was moving faster, and people were ready for faster music.

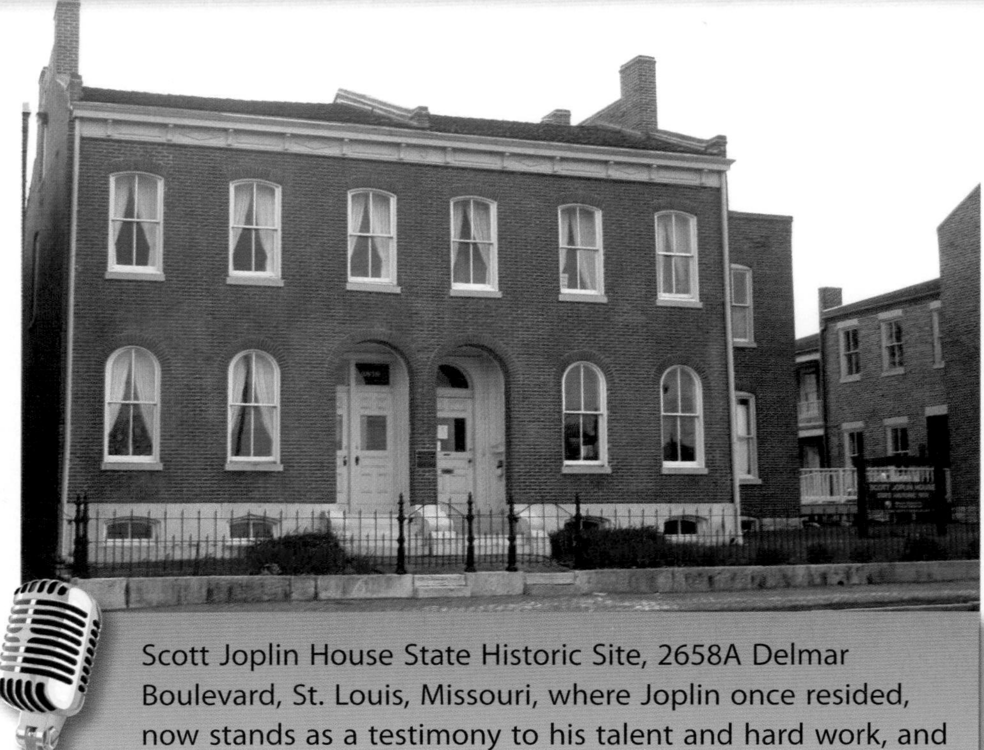

Scott Joplin House State Historic Site, 2658A Delmar Boulevard, St. Louis, Missouri, where Joplin once resided, now stands as a testimony to his talent and hard work, and also includes museum exhibits that interpret Joplin's life.

The same was true for the United States on the world stage. After defeating Spain in the Spanish-American War, the United States had become one of the most powerful countries in the world. The country was filled with energy and excitement. It was ready for a fast-paced musical style, and ragtime was a perfect fit.

At home, the family piano had become very important. The piano was a family's entertainment center. Before automobiles became popular, a piano was a family's second-biggest purchase after a house. Owning a piano was a sign of success—a sign that the family had "made it." Buying sheet music for the piano was the way Americans brought music into their homes. More and more now, that music was ragtime.

Surrounded by music as he was in Sedalia, Joplin had plenty of chances to play. He played the cornet and piano at a variety of places,

A cornet

and he also formed the Texas Medley Quartette with his brothers Will and Robert. Despite its name, this group actually had eight members. It toured as far east as Syracuse, New York.

It was in Syracuse that Joplin published his first two songs: "Please Say You Will" in February 1895, and "A Picture of Her Face" that July. Neither, however, are rags. They are slow ballads.

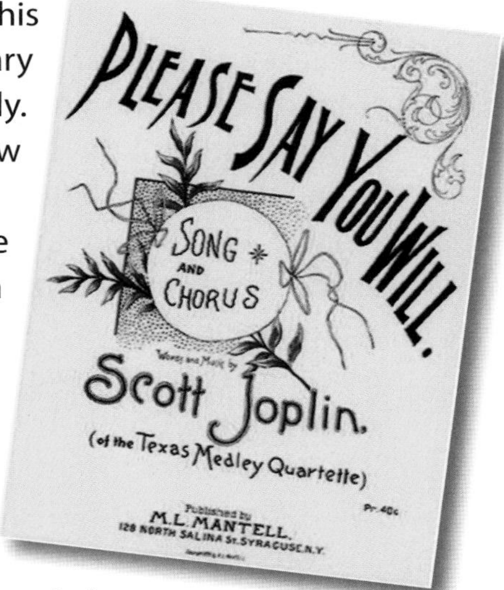
Please Say You Will.
Song and Chorus
Words and Music by
Scott Joplin.
(of the Texas Medley Quartette)
Published by
M.L. MANTELL.
128 NORTH SALINA St. SYRACUSE N.Y.

The following year Joplin published three more songs. One was a waltz and one a march. The third, called "Great Crush Collision March," was based on an actual public relations stunt. During the Crush Collision, two locomotives purposely slammed into each other, headfirst at full speed, while 50,000 people watched. The spectacle turned disastrous: Three people were killed and dozens more were injured when the engine boilers exploded.

"Great Crush Collision March" is the first of Joplin's published songs to contain elements of ragtime. He used the piano to make train-whistle noises. He also pretended the piano was the two trains, playing the song in a fast style that got even faster as the two engines approached each other. He probably also used a ragged beat—another element of ragtime.

Chapter 3

Joplin liked teaching others how to play the piano. He was always smiling and always ready with a kind word to those just starting out. Samuel Campbell studied with Joplin and later described him: "He liked a little beer, and gambled some, but he never let such things interfere with his music. . . . He was then about twenty-nine years old . . . about five feet seven inches tall; a good dresser, usually neat, but sometimes a little careless with his clothes; gentlemanly and pleasant, with a liking for companionship."[3]

Joplin enrolled, sometime in the mid-late 1890s, in the Smith College of Music. The school was part of the local George R. Smith College for Negroes. To make money while attending school, Joplin played in bars and casinos in and around Sedalia.

One place that Joplin played and also attended as a customer was a club for African Americans called the Black 400 Club. The club featured the cakewalk—a dance people did with great movement, making fun of fancy balls. The cakewalk needed music like ragtime—upbeat and bouncy, with unique sounds and chords.

In November 1898, another African-American club opened in Sedalia: the Maple Leaf Club. Around this same time Joplin had completed the rag that would make him famous, and to which his name would forever be linked: "Maple Leaf Rag." While it may sound logical to assume it was named after the club, there are other possible explanations: One is that it was named for the many maple trees in Sedalia; another is that it was named after a popular song of the time called "Maple Leaf Waltz."

Even the story of how it was published is a mystery. One says that one hot summer day, the owner of a music store, John Stark, stopped by the Maple Leaf Club for something cold to drink. From somewhere in the club came the sound of music. Stark followed the sound and saw Joplin at the piano playing "Maple Leaf Rag." Stark decided to publish the song. However, Joplin historian Edward A. Berlin doubts this explanation. For one reason, in these days before air conditioning, many clubs were closed in the summer.

Another story has Joplin coming into Stark's store and asking him to publish it. Stark declines, saying it's too hard to play so no one will buy it. Joplin then leaves and comes back moments later with an African-American boy, who sits down at the piano and plays the song perfectly. His performance convinces Stark to publish it. Another version of this tale has the boy dancing enthusiastically to the song, and Stark then agreeing to publish it. Another story is that Joplin's attorney, R. A. Higdon, arranged the deal with Stark. The problem with these stories, as Berlin points out, is that Stark was not known as a music publisher at this time.

No matter which story is true, Stark did agree to publish the song. The contract was unusual in that it gave Joplin an advance of $50 plus a one-cent royalty (a payment for each copy of the song that sold), rather than just buying the song outright. Some say that this was the first time a music composer earned royalties on a song.

"Maple Leaf Rag" was not a huge seller at first; the first year Joplin made just $4 from royalties over the $50 advance.[4] However, people talked about it. The more they talked, the more popular it became. It was heard in music stores, taverns, and nightclubs. By 1905 it was selling at the rate of 3,000 copies per month, and Joplin was making around $600 a year—the same as a factory worker then.[5]

A mural of Scott Joplin adorns a building in Sedalia, Missouri. Joplin was not a flashy piano player. He even wrote instructions on some of his songs to play them slow, because he thought that playing ragtime too fast ruined it.

Musicians loved to play the song. "I played [it] a lot. . . . I think it is one of the finest tunes ever written,"[6] said composer J. Russel Robinson.

"Maple Leaf Rag" established Joplin's reputation as the King of Ragtime. Would he be able to keep his crown?

John Stark

John Stillwell Stark was born in Kentucky on April 11, 1841. His family later moved to a farm in Indiana. John served in the Union Army during the Civil War. He then worked as a farmer and ice-cream maker.

Stark married in 1865, right after the war, and in 1882 he moved his family to Sedalia, Missouri. There, he opened a small music store, bought out a competitor, and called the business John Stark and Son.

After the success of "Maple Leaf Rag," Stark decided to focus solely on publishing ragtime tunes. He published some of the music's most popular composers, including Joseph Lamb, James Scott, and Arthur Marshall.

In 1905 Stark opened an office in New York City. He, along with Joplin, supported "classic" ragtime and not the newer, fast-paced style. (Stark himself coined the term *classic rag*.) He helped to spread the popularity of ragtime beyond African-American audiences.

For the first few years, Stark and Joplin had a very successful partnership. Unfortunately, after several business disagreements, they ended their relationship around 1910.

When his wife died later that year, Stark returned to the Midwest. He continued publishing rags by other composers, even after the music had lost its popularity. According to his official Missouri death certificate, he died in St. Louis on October 21, 1927.[7]

John Stillwell Stark

Chapter 4

his love of music prevented delinquency. As a small boy, he
had formed a little band with four other boys and their home-
made instruments, serenading on New Orleans corners for
pennies. Louis's mouth was very big. His pockets were very
raggedy—pennies might fall through. But his mouth could
hold quite a few pennies. Early in life, Louis acquired the name
Satchelmouth, shortened eventually to Satchmo. Sometimes
his friends called him Dippermouth, too. He had a bright, good-
natured smile, all the wider because his mouth was so large.
And even as a little boy, selling the Times-Picayune at a news-
stand on a busy Canal Street corner, Louis had a deep gravelly
SCOTT JOPLIN
COMPOSER

Struggle for Respectability

The success of "Maple Leaf Rag" made Joplin a celebrity. During a time of widespread racial prejudice, this was a big achievement. Ragtime, however, did not fare as well. To many Americans, ragtime was pigeonholed as "black music," played in seedy bars by honky-tonk piano players.

Joplin was determined to change that view. He desperately wanted ragtime to be respected by wider audiences. That would make African-American music respectable, and, in turn, make African Americans more respectable.

Joplin was confident and happy. Day after day, he sat at his piano, working out his next musical composition. He'd try different combinations of notes and capture them on paper. Sometimes he'd write down what he thought he liked, only to play the notes later and scratch them out. It was a long, slow process.

Meanwhile he was trying to write an incredibly ambitious work called "The Ragtime Dance." It had an orchestra, a master of ceremonies, and four dancing couples. It was more like a small opera than a song.

Joplin was determined to show that a ragtime musician like himself could write other types of music. In the late autumn of 1899, he rented the Woods' Opera House in Sedalia to put on a performance of "The Ragtime Dance." He hoped to get people interested in the work and to convince Stark to publish it. Stark thought the piece was too complicated and declined. Joplin tried to interest other music publishers without success.

By this time ragtime was gaining popularity in the United States, although it still had many critics. It is possible that racism fueled the criticism. Some said it would ruin American kids and destroy their desire for "good" music. Ragtime was called "cheap, trashy stuff" and a "national calamity."[1]

Joplin realized that he had outgrown Sedalia. He needed to move to a bigger city to advance his career. So in the spring of 1901 he moved to St. Louis, where ragtime was very popular. Belle Hayden, a widow he had fallen in love with in Sedalia, went with him. Shortly after they arrived in the city they got married. They moved into a second-floor apartment on Morgan Town Road.

The town's newspaper, the *St. Louis Globe-Democrat,* ran a big story on him. He also had many friends in the city. He listed himself in the telephone book simply as "Joplin, Scott, music."

But that's how Joplin was. He was quiet and shy. He didn't brag or boast about the success he had achieved. "He never talked very much," remembered a woman who knew him at this time. "He was a very quiet man."[2]

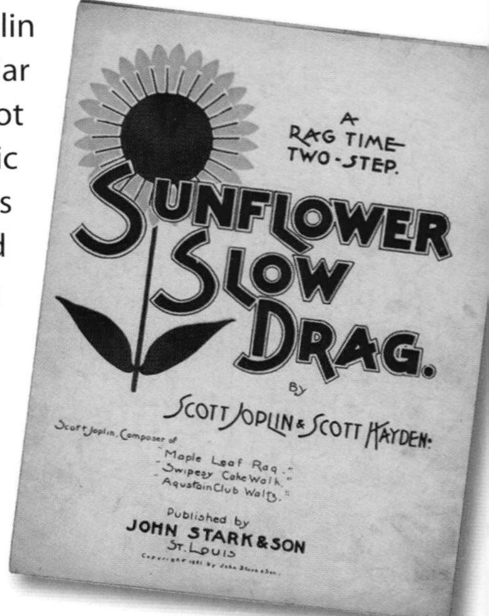

Even when he played the piano, Joplin was not flashy. It was becoming popular to play ragtime very fast. This was not Joplin's way. (Sometimes on his music compositions he would write warnings not to play the song fast.) Others showed off while playing. So now, unlike in Sedalia, he often lost in piano-playing contests.

Now that Joplin was married, he tried just writing and teaching music rather than playing all around town. He continued getting songs published, such as "Sunflower Slow Drag" and

"Peacherine Rag." In October 1901 he self-published "The Easy Winners," and in early 1902 other music publishers released two more of his songs.

Joplin probably used other publishers as a way to show Stark that he didn't need him, so Stark had better keep him happy by publishing "The Ragtime Dance." Eventually Stark did publish it, but just as he thought, it was too long and too difficult for most people to play on the piano. It sold poorly.

By the end of 1902 Joplin had published eight pieces of music, including "The Entertainer"—a song that was later featured in the movie *The Sting*. It was popular when it was first released, and today it is Joplin's most famous work. One writer called it "a jingling work of a very original character."[3]

However, even as Joplin's professional life was going well, his personal life was not. Sometime before 1903, his brother Will died. In addition, he and his wife weren't getting along; she had no interest in music.

In early 1903, though, the couple had a baby girl. With her birth, there was hope for their relationship. When the baby died a few months later, Scott and his wife were devastated. Their marriage could not endure the pain, and they separated a few months later.

Even though "The Ragtime Dance" hadn't sold well, Joplin wrote a ragtime opera called *A Guest of Honor*. Again, Stark didn't want to publish it because it was too long and difficult to play.

Joplin really wanted *A Guest of Honor* to be successful. He assembled a cast of 32 people and called them Scott Joplin's Ragtime Opera

Chapter 4

PAUL NEWMAN · ROBERT REDFORD
ROBERT SHAW
IN A BILL/PHILLIPS PRODUCTION OF
A GEORGE ROY HILL FILM
THE STING
A RICHARD D. ZANUCK/DAVID BROWN PRESENTATION
...all it takes is a little Confidence.
Written by
DAVID S. WARD
Directed by
GEORGE ROY HILL
Produced by
TONY BILL, MICHAEL and JULIA PHILLIPS
Music Adapted by MARVIN HAMLISCH · A UNIVERSAL PICTURE · TECHNICOLOR®
ORIGINAL SOUNDTRACK AVAILABLE EXCLUSIVELY ON MCA RECORDS AND TAPES
PG

The 1973 movie *The Sting* made Scott Joplin a household name across America. It was an immensely popular film, and Joplin's music played a major role in its success.

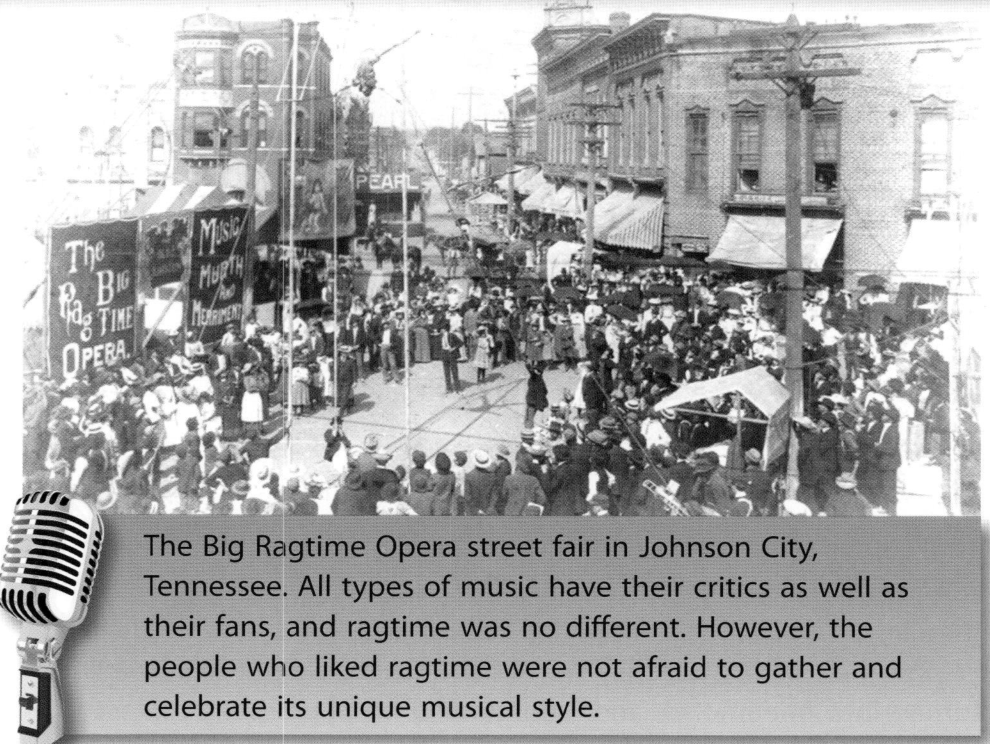

The Big Ragtime Opera street fair in Johnson City, Tennessee. All types of music have their critics as well as their fans, and ragtime was no different. However, the people who liked ragtime were not afraid to gather and celebrate its unique musical style.

Company. The group went to Midwestern cities in September 1903 to perform the opera.

Unfortunately, the tour ended in disaster. While it is uncertain why the opera company had to stop performing, some people think that Joplin had a trunk taken away when he could not pay a bill (the trunk was taken as payment). The trunk likely contained unpublished music, manuscripts, and other important items, including the score for *A Guest of Honor.* (To this day, no copy of the opera has been found.)

When Joplin returned to St. Louis, he was nearly broke, his marriage was over, and his opera was a disaster. He decided to move back to Sedalia, where the memories were better. He never mentioned *A Guest of Honor* again, but the opera bug remained in his system.

Despite his troubles, Joplin was still creative. In 1904 he wrote one of his finest pieces: "The Cascades." It was based on the Cascades Gardens, a huge display of waterfalls and water fountains at the 1904 St. Louis Fair.

Another piece Joplin published that year was "The Chrysanthemum," which was based on a dream he had after reading *Alice in Wonderland*. He dedicated the song to a nineteen-year-old woman named Freddie Alexander. Joplin had met her during a trip to Texarkana early in 1904 to visit relatives. They fell in love, and the two were married in Little Rock, Arkansas, on June 14.

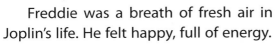

Freddie was a breath of fresh air in Joplin's life. He felt happy, full of energy. The sun felt warm and good on his face, and the songs of birds sounded extra sweet. He was in love, and it was better than anything that had happened to him for a while.

But then, soon after they were married, Freddie got sick. The illness turned into pneumonia, and Freddie died on September 10, less than three months after they were married.

Once again the light had gone out in Joplin's life. He must have sat there, in their apartment, grief-stricken beyond words. Did he turn to his music in this hour of need? Or did the piano sit, dusty and unused? No one knows.

In 1905, John Stark moved his business to New York City, the music publishing capital of the world. Joplin kicked around the Midwest for a few more years, but likely knew in his heart that New York was the place for him to be as well if he wanted to further his career.

Before he left the Midwest, however, Joplin visited his family in Texarkana once more, early in 1907. His mother had died, but his father was still alive. Joplin was treated like a celebrity. He played the piano at several events, and told stories about the places he'd been and the people he'd met. The family couldn't get enough of him. "They [the family] kept him up all day till late at night," said Joplin's nephew Fred.[4]

When Joplin left for New York City, he would never again return to the Midwest.

Ragtime's Big Three

Two composers who are often mentioned in the same breath as Joplin are Joseph Lamb and James Scott. Together with Joplin, they make up ragtime's "Big Three."

Joseph Lamb was born in Montclair, New Jersey, on December 6, 1887. He went to college to study engineering, but his interest in music soon outweighed his passion for his college studies. He left school in the autumn of 1904 and worked a series of odd jobs. All the time he was growing more and more fond of Joplin's rags. In 1907 he was at Stark's store in New York City to buy some music. He mentioned to Mrs. Stark how much he admired Joplin, and she pointed to Joplin sitting quietly in the corner. The two talked, and later Lamb played one of his compositions entitled "Sensation." Joplin convinced Stark to publish it, and it was an instant hit.

For a decade Lamb was a major composer of rags. However, he never wanted to make music his career, and instead became an accountant. He enjoyed new popularity in the late 1950s, composed some new rags, and even made some recordings. He died on September 3, 1960.

James Scott was born in Neosho, Missouri, on February 12, 1885. Both of his parents were former slaves. He got a job at the music store of Charlie Dumars in 1902. At first he strictly performed menial tasks, but his musical abilities kept shining through, and soon he was playing his own songs.

In 1906 James Scott met Scott Joplin. Joplin liked his rags and took him to Stark. Scott's first composition, "Frog Legs Rag," was a hit, and thereafter Stark published over twenty of Scott's songs. In later years Scott played piano in movie theaters to accompany silent films. He died in Kansas City, Kansas, in 1938.

Chapter 5

The New York Years

When Joplin moved to New York City in the summer of 1907, he lived one block from Broadway in an area called the Tenderloin. The Tenderloin was the entertainment center of the city. As Joplin walked down the street, he saw theaters, restaurants, saloons, clubs, and gambling houses all located close to each other. Customers—both black and white—came and went at all hours of the day and night. The area was alive with sound—horse-drawn carriages clopping by; people walking up and down the street, talking, shouting, laughing and crying; even brand-new motorcars puttering by, their engines making a racket.

Just one block from Joplin's address was Tin Pan Alley, home to numerous music publishers. There were so many pianos playing music in that area that it sounded as if people were banging on tin pans, which gave the area its name.

New York City was alive with an energy all its own. Immigrants were pouring into the city, new buildings were being built, and the streets were booming with people. There was always something going on. The city was abuzz with the sounds of many different languages.

The energy of the city seemed to inspire Joplin. Eight pieces of music were published with his name in 1907. Some were individual songs, and some were collaborations. He was producing music and he had money. A friend said that he "was dressed up like a Fancy Dan of ragtime, sporting diamonds."[1]

Chapter 5

In the early 1900s, Tin Pan Alley was the center of the music publishing industry. At this time, it was located on West 28th Street between 5th and 6th Avenues in New York City. All types and styles of music wafted from the windows, mixing together in one incredible roar of sound.

Things got even better for Joplin when he met a thirty-three-year-old woman named Lottie Stokes. She provided love and a stable environment for him. In later years she said that they got married. However, there are no papers, such as a marriage license, to prove that. It is possible that they had a common-law marriage (one in which two people agree to live together as husband and wife even though they are not legally married).

Despite its popularity, ragtime music still had many critics. Joplin tried to answer those critics in 1908 in a booklet he wrote called *The School of Ragtime*. It contained six piano exercises teaching the "correct" way to play ragtime. In the booklet's introduction, Joplin wrote: "[R]agtime . . . is here to stay. . . . [R]eal ragtime of the higher class is rather difficult to play. . . . [S]yncopations are no indication of light or trashy music."[2]

Still trying to do something more "respectable," Joplin began writing *Treemonisha*. A news article that appeared on March 5, 1908, was full of praise for Joplin and his new project. "Critics who have heard a part of his new opera are very optimistic as to its future success," it said.[3]

One person who was not happy about Joplin's opera was John Stark. After the failure of "The Ragtime Dance" and the battle over *A Guest of Honor,* Stark was in no mood to hear about another Joplin opera. At this time the music publishing industry was difficult. Larger companies were taking over the smaller ones and pricing their sheet music below what the smaller publishers could. Even if he wanted to publish *Treemonisha,* Stark probably could not have afforded to do so.

Stark had other problems. His wife was sick, and the medical bills were growing. This likely caused Stark to ask Joplin to accept a one-time payment for the sale of his future rags, rather than continuing the royalty agreement that the two had had for years. Joplin was angry about Stark's lack of enthusiasm for *Treemonisha*. He refused Stark's offer of no more royalties. Stark got angry and swore that he'd never publish any more of Joplin's work.

In 1909 Joplin had a creative burst. He published six songs, all with the Seminary Music Company. However, he had other problems to consider. Ragtime was starting to fade as two new music styles—jazz and the blues—were replacing it. Maybe that's why Joplin pushed so hard to try to finish something greater than a rag. He knew that time was running out for ragtime. Since people associated him with ragtime, maybe time was running out for him too.

By the autumn of 1910, Joplin had finished *Treemonisha*. Now came the familiar problem: Trying to find a music publisher. "What headaches that caused him!"[4] remembered Lottie.

Once again, Joplin was unsuccessful. Day after day he left his home carrying the opera manuscript, hopeful that he could find a buyer. He'd visit each of the music publishers, manuscript in hand, and explain why they should publish it. Normally soft-spoken and quiet, one can imagine his eyes sparkling and his voice rising excitedly as he talked about the work he had poured so much of himself into. But the answer was always the same.

Joplin was determined not to let *Treemonisha* fail. He continually rewrote and revised it. Around June of 1913 he announced a production of *Treemonisha*—now called a comic opera—in Bayou (Bayonne), New Jersey. However, the performance either never happened, or it was so poorly received that the newspapers didn't cover it.

Ragtime was continuing to fall out of favor. Joplin tried to defend it in a letter to the *Age* in 1913: "When composers put decent words to ragtime melodies there will be very little kicking from the public about ragtime,"[5] he wrote, but he might as well have tried to stop water from rushing through his fingers. Ragtime as a popular music form was on its way out, and he couldn't stop it.

By that time Joplin may have already been feeling the effects of a terrible disease that he had contracted: syphilis. But if indeed he was feeling ill, he ignored it and pushed ahead. In October 1913, he established the Scott Joplin Music Publishing Company, with Lottie as co-owner.

The following year he published the song "Magnetic Rag." It is one of his best songs. It is also the last piece he would write and publish, although others that he wrote earlier would be published in later years.

A 2010 performance of *Treemonisha* at the Théâtre du Châtelet in Paris, France. In 1972, fifty-five years after Joplin's death, the Afro-American Music Workshop of Morehouse College produced the first formal staging of *Treemonisha* at the Atlanta [Georgia] Memorial Arts Center. Audiences loved it. Today Joplin's opera is considered a masterpiece, and it is staged all over the world.

"Magnetic Rag" shows that even though his disease was progressing, he was continuing to grow as a musician. The song is influenced by the different sounds and cultures that he encountered every day in the city. At age forty-six, sick and slowing down, Joplin was still a master musician.

Toward the end of 1914, Joplin and Lottie moved to 133 West 138th Street in Harlem. Money was growing short. He put a notice in the newspaper that he would accept violin and piano students. In February 1915 he published another notice that he would send six copies of any type of popular music to anyone who sent him one dollar.

By the later months of 1915, Joplin's syphilis was destroying his motor skills; his eye-hand coordination was nearly gone. Jazz pianist Eubie Blake recalled seeing Joplin at this time painfully trying to play "Maple Leaf Rag": "So pitiful. He . . . sounded like a little child trying to pick out a tune."[6]

How frustrating this must have been for Joplin! The piano, always his friend in the past, had become his enemy. How discouraged, and how frightened, he must have felt as he tried to get his fingers to move over the keys the way he wanted them to.

To add to his problems, money was extremely tight. A friend recalled how Joplin traveled from Harlem to the Bronx just to get an old coat and a hat that were offered to him.

In October 1916, Joplin announced that he was going to his sister's home in Chicago to recover from a serious illness. He never made the journey. By this time the syphilis was affecting his mind. Lottie said that he destroyed many of his unpublished songs because he believed they were going to be stolen. Finally he lost the power to speak so that he could be understood.

At the end of January 1917, Joplin entered New York's Bellevue Hospital. Shortly thereafter he was transferred to a mental ward at Manhattan State Hospital. It was there he died on April 1, 1917, at age 49. He had asked that "Maple Leaf Rag" be played at his funeral, but Lottie said no because she didn't consider it the right kind of music for a funeral.

"Boy, when I'm dead twenty-five years, people are going to begin to recognize me,"[7] Joplin once said. In one respect he was right. Beginning in the 1970s there was a renewed interest in his music. In another sense he was incorrect, for he was a brilliant musician, and the music he left behind remains alive. Like all great musicians, Scott Joplin has never been, and will never be, forgotten.

The Ragtime Revival

It took some time for Scott Joplin to get noticed. It took a 1973 movie to bring Joplin to light once again.

In the late 1960s and early 1970s, records came out of ragtime tunes, including Joplin songs. Film director George Roy Hill heard one of these ragtime albums and decided the music would be perfect for his upcoming film *The Sting*. The movie was about a group of con artists who plan an elaborate money swindle on a criminal. The movie was a big success. It won seven Oscars, including Best Picture. Joplin's music, adapted by Marvin Hamlisch, won the Oscar for Best Film Score. The song used most often throughout the film was Joplin's "The Entertainer."

The immense popularity of the film opened the floodgates for ragtime. "The Entertainer" was heard everywhere, from supermarket loudspeakers to weddings. Recordings of Joplin songs flooded the marketplace. In 1975, *Treemonisha* played for eight weeks on Broadway in New York City.

The awards kept coming. In 1976 Joplin received a posthumous Pulitzer Prize—the most important award in the world of writing. The following year a film about his life, starring Billy Dee Williams, was released. Then, in 1983, the United States Postal Service issued a Joplin stamp. He was inducted into the Songwriters Hall of Fame.

The Joplin/ragtime frenzy has died down again, but they are now both firmly part of the American music scene.

1867 or **1868** Scott Joplin is born to Florence Givens and Giles Joplin.

1874 or **1875** Scott knows how to play the banjo.

c. 1883 Joplin forms a vocal group with several others in Texarkana, possibly including his brother Robert. He also plays the piano in local dance halls and teaches guitar and mandolin.

c. 1887 Joplin leaves Texarkana and eventually settles in Sedalia, Missouri.

1893 Joplin plays at the Columbian Exposition (the World's Fair) in Chicago.

1895 He publishes his first two songs: "Please Say You Will" in February and "A Picture of Her Face" in July.

1896 He publishes "Great Crush Collision March," the first song to be considered ragtime.

c. 1897 Joplin enrolls in the Smith College of Music, part of the local George R. Smith College for Negroes.

1899 John Stark hears Joplin play "Maple Leaf Rag" and publishes the sheet music for $50 advance against royalties of one cent per copy. Joplin rents the Woods' Opera House in Sedalia to perform "The Ragtime Dance."

1901 He moves to St. Louis with his new wife, the widow Belle Hayden.

1902 "The Ragtime Dance" is published.

1903 In September, he assembles a cast of 32 people and calls them Scott Joplin's Ragtime Opera Company. Their plan is to perform *A Guest of Honor* across the Midwest, but misfortune renders the company broke.

1904 Joplin writes "The Cascades," based on the Cascades Gardens, a huge display of waterfalls and water fountains at the 1904 St. Louis Fair; and "The Chrysanthemum," based on a dream he had after reading *Alice in Wonderland.* On June 14 he marries Freddie Alexander; she dies of pneumonia September 10.

1907 Joplin spends time in Chicago with Louis Chauven, writing "Heliotrope Bouquet," and in New York, meeting new publishers and getting to know composer Joseph Lamb.

1908 *The School of Ragtime: Six Exercises for Piano* is published.

1911 Joplin stages a low-budget performance of *Treemonisha* to entice investors.

1913 With Lottie Stokes, Joplin forms the Scott Joplin Music Publishing Company.

1914 The Scott Joplin Music Publishing Company issues "Magnetic Rag."

1917 Joplin dies from complications of syphilis on April 1.

1973 *The Sting,* an award-winning movie starring Paul Newman and Robert Redford and featuring Joplin's "The Entertainer," is released.

1975 *Treemonisha* is performed on Broadway.

1976 Joplin is awarded a Pulitzer Prize.

1983 The U.S. Postal Service issues a postage stamp honoring Scott Joplin.

1895	"A Picture of Her Face"
1895	"Please Say You Will"
1896	"Great Crush Collision March"
1899	"Maple Leaf Rag"
1899	"Original Rags"
1901	"Peacherine Rag"
1902	"The Ragtime Dance"
	"A Breeze From Alabama"
	"Elite Syncopations"
	"The Entertainer"
1903	*A Guest of Honor* (opera)
	"Palm Leaf"
	"Weeping Willow"
1904	"The Chrysanthemum"
1905	"Eugenia"
1907	"Heliotrope Bouquet"
	"Nonpareil"
1908	"Fig Leaf Rag"
	The School of Ragtime: Six Exercises for Piano
1909	"Country Club"
1910	"Stoptime Rag"
1911	*Treemonisha* (opera)
	"Felicity Rag"
1912	"Scott Joplin's New Rag"
1913	"Kismet"
1914	"Magnetic Rag"
1917	"Reflection Rag"

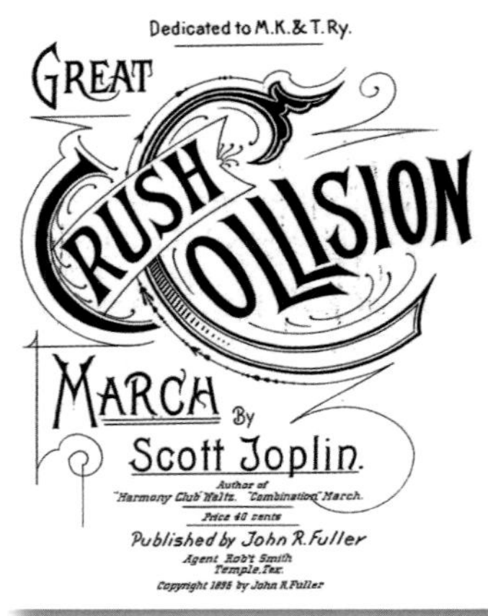

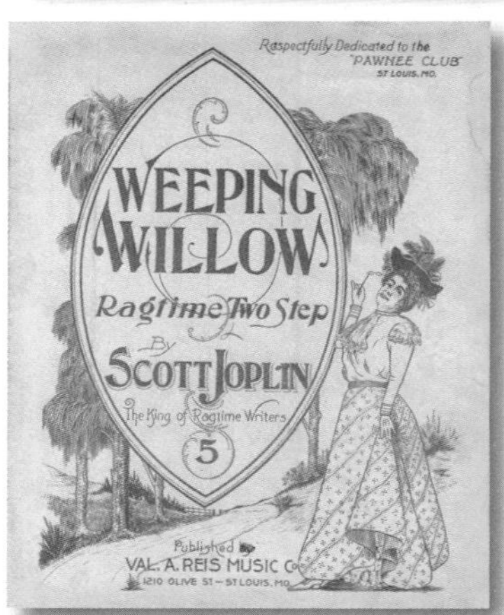

Chapter One. *Treemonisha*

1. Edward A. Berlin, *King of Ragtime* (New York: Oxford University Press, 1994), p. 214.
2. Ibid., p. 45.

Chapter Two. A Boy with a Gift

1. Edward A. Berlin, *King of Ragtime* (New York: Oxford University Press, 1994), p. 4.
2. Ibid., p. 6.
3. Peter Gammond, *Scott Joplin and the Ragtime Era* (New York: St. Martin's Press, 1975), p. 29.
4. James Haskins, *Scott Joplin* (New York: Doubleday & Company, Inc., 1978), p. 60.
5. Berlin, p. 8.
6. *Ragtime,* edited by John Edward Hasse (New York: Schirmer Books, 1985), p. 8.
7. Pathways to Freedom: Maryland and the Underground Railroad, "Music," http://pathways.thinkport.org/secrets/music1.cfm

Chapter Three. "Maple Leaf Rag"

1. Edward A. Berlin, *King of Ragtime* (New York: Oxford University Press, 1994), 13.
2. *Ragtime,* edited by John Edward Hasse (New York: Schirmer Books, 1985), p. 9.
3. James Haskins, *Scott Joplin* (New York: Doubleday & Company, Inc., 1978), p. 89.
4. Ibid., p. 102.
5. Berlin, p. 58.
6. Ibid., p. 56.
7. Missouri State Board of Health: Certificate of Death for John S. Stark; http://www.sos.mo.gov/images/archives/deathcerts/1927/1927_00032764.PDF

Chapter Four. Struggle for Respectability

1. Edward A. Berlin, *King of Ragtime* (New York: Oxford University Press, 1994), p. 43.
2. Ibid., p. 97.
3. Ibid., p. 107.
4. James Haskins, *Scott Joplin* (New York: Doubleday & Company, Inc., 1978), p. 150.

Chapter Five. The New York Years

1. Edward A. Berlin, *King of Ragtime* (New York: Oxford University Press, 1994), p. 176.
2. James Haskins, *Scott Joplin* (New York: Doubleday & Company, Inc., 1978), p. 159.
3. Ibid., p. 162.
4. Ibid., p. 172.
5. Haskins, p. 186.
6. David A. Jasen and Gene Jones, *Black Bottom Stomp* (New York: Routledge, 2002), p. 29.
7. Berlin, p. 3.

Further Reading

BOOKS

Gann, Marjorie, and Janet Willen. *Five Thousand Years of Slavery.* Toronto, Canada: Tundra Books, 2011.

Hoffman, Mary Ann. *Scott Joplin: King of Ragtime.* New York: Gareth Stevens, 2010.

Platt, Richard. *Through Time: New York City.* New York: Kingfisher, 2010.

Sullivan, Sarah. *Passing the Music Down.* Somerville, Mass.: Candlewick, 2011.

WORKS CONSULTED

Berlin, Edward A. *King of Ragtime.* New York: Oxford University Press, 1994.

———. *Ragtime.* Berkeley: University of California Press, 1980.

Gammond, Peter. *Scott Joplin and the Ragtime Era.* New York: St. Martin's Press, 1975.

Haskins, James. *Scott Joplin.* New York: Doubleday & Company, Inc., 1978.

Jasen, David A., and Gene Jones. *Black Bottom Stomp.* New York: Routledge, 2002.

Jasen, David A., and Trebor Jay Tichenor. *Rags and Ragtime: A Musical History.* New York: The Seabury Press, 1978.

Pathways to Freedom: Maryland and the Underground Railroad. http://pathways.thinkport.org/flash_home.cfm

Ragtime: Its History, Composers, Music. Edited by John Edward Hasse. New York: Schirmer Books, 1985.

ON THE INTERNET

MusicOrb.com
http://www.musicorb.com/

"Perfesser" Bill Edwards's Ragtime Resource Center
http://www.perfessorbill.com/

Ragtime Music
http://www.ragtimemusic.com/

The Scott Joplin International Ragtime Festival
http://www.scottjoplin.org/

West Coast Ragtime Society
http://www.westcoastragtime.com/

PHOTO CREDITS: Cover—Joe Rasemas; pp. 4, 34—Hulton Archive/Getty Images; pp. 13, 19, 23, 42—Library of Congress; p. 14—Corbis-Bettman; pp. 15, 18, 19 (top), 26, 27, 28, 29—cc-by-sa; pp. 16, 22, 25, 32, 41—Barbara Marvis; p. 37—Joel Saget/AFP/Getty Images . Every effort has been made to locate all copyright holders of material used in this book. If any errors or omissions have occurred, corrections will be made in future editions of the book.

advance (ad-VANTZ)—Money paid for a project against royalties earned.

ambitious (am-BIH-shus)—Challenging; showing or requiring a lot of effort.

bankroll (BANK-roll)—To provide money for a venture or cause.

blues (BLOOZ)—A type of sad music that developed from the songs of black slaves in the South.

casino (kuh-SEE-noh)—A place used for gambling.

cornet (kor-NET)—A brass instrument similar to but smaller than a trumpet.

flamboyant (flam-BOY-ant)—Showy.

haphazard (hap-HAZ-ard)—Lacking order.

jazz (JAZ)—A type of music that developed from the blues to have a strong, lively beat and for which players often make up musical phrases on the spot.

mandolin (MAN-doh-lin)—A musical instrument with a guitar-like neck and a pear-shaped wooden body.

pigeonhole (PID-jun-hohl)—To put aside; to put in an often narrow category.

prejudice (PREH-joo-diss)—Hostile attitude against a particular group.

quartette (kwar-TET)—A group of four (usually spelled *quartet*).

royalty (ROY-ul-tee)—A payment promised for each copy sold; when enough copies of the project have been sold to match the advance, further royalties can be paid.

syphilis (SIH-fih-lis)—A contagious disease that causes sores on and in the body; left untreated, it eventually affects vital organs, including the brain, and leads to death.

Index

About the Author

Russell Roberts has written and published nearly 40 books for adults and children, including *C.C. Sabathia, Larry Fitzgerald, The Building of the Panama Canal, The Cyclopes, The Minotaur, The Battle of Hastings*, and *The Battle of Waterloo.* He lives in Bordentown, New Jersey, with his family and a fat, fuzzy, and crafty calico cat named Rusti.